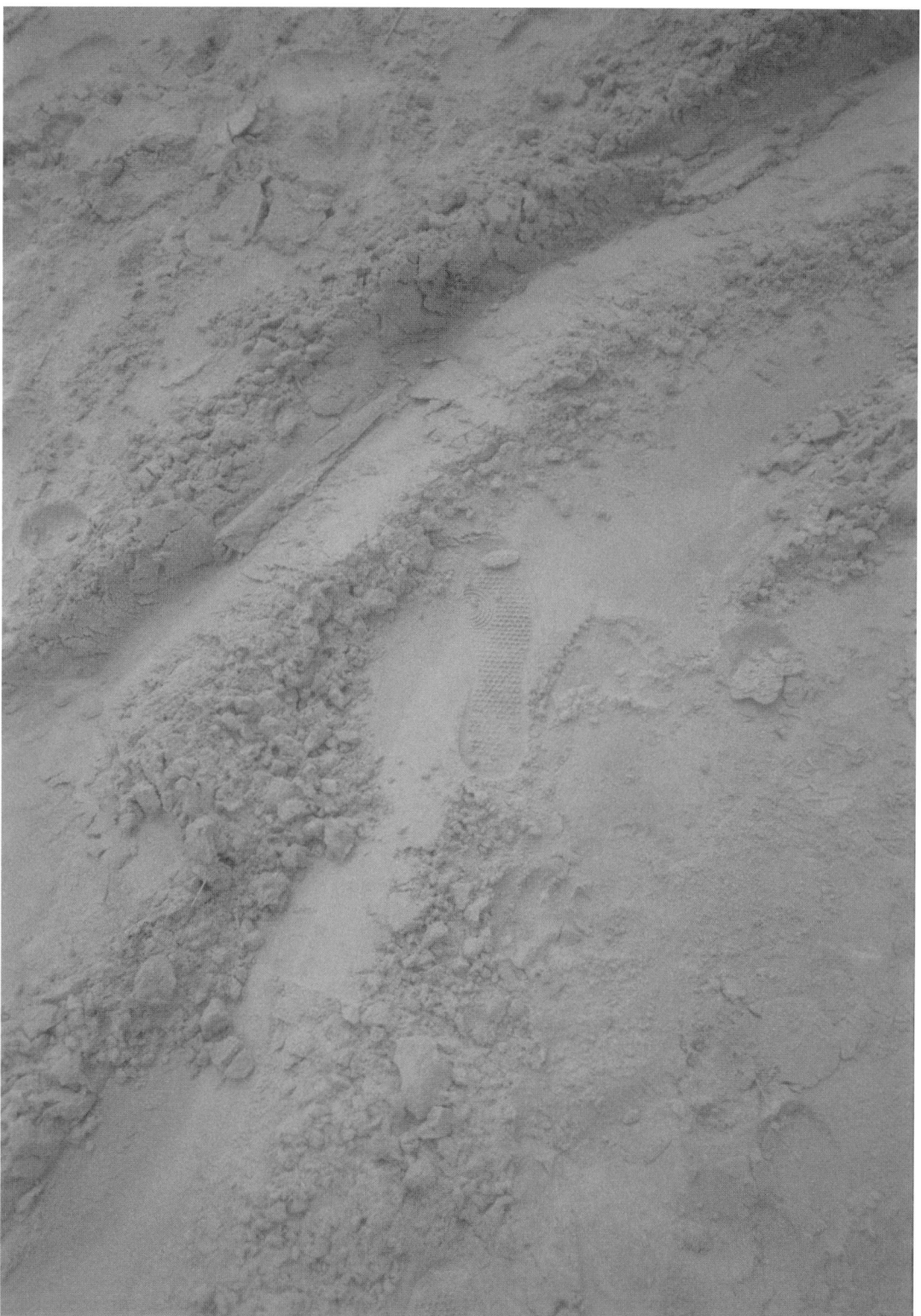

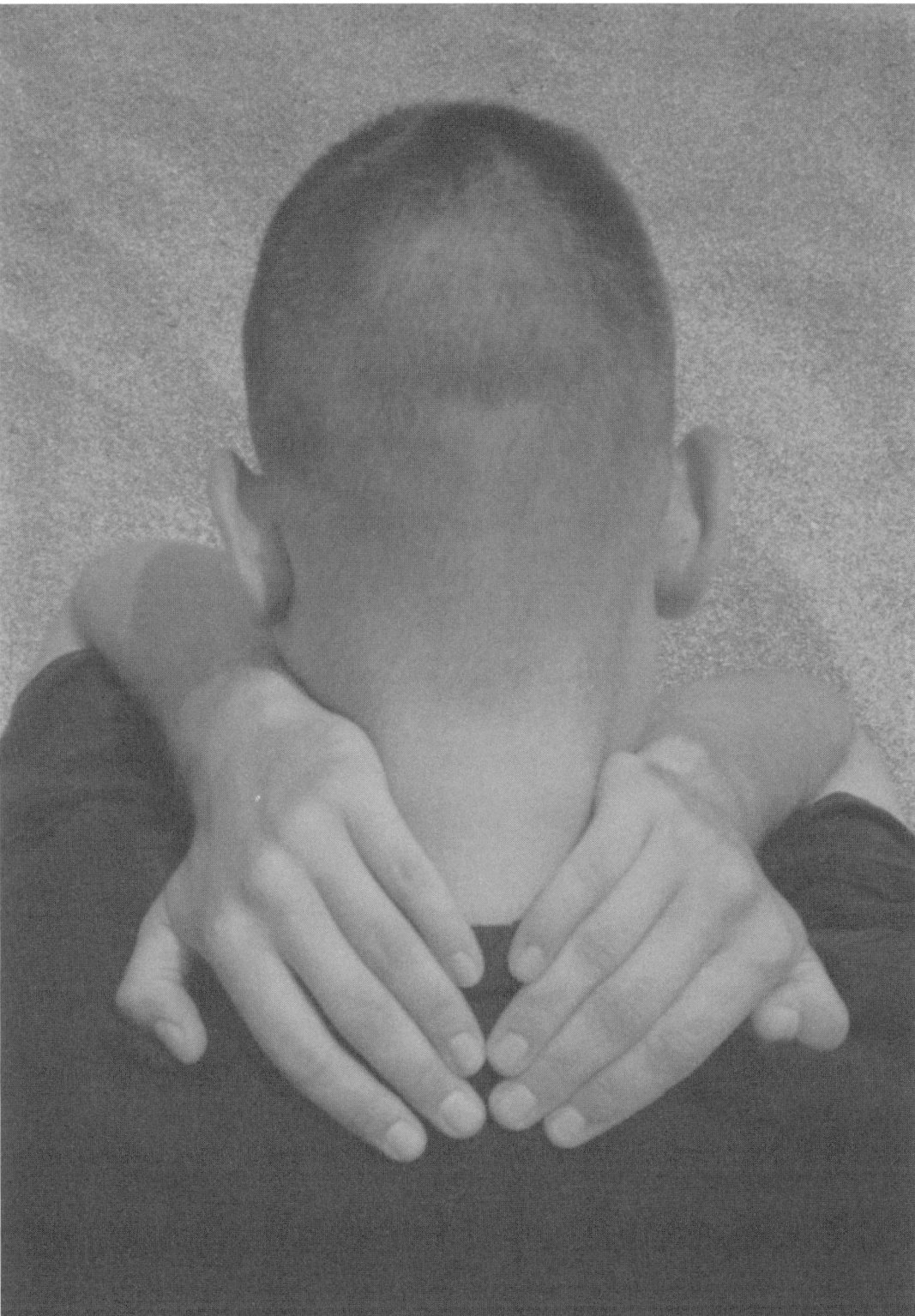

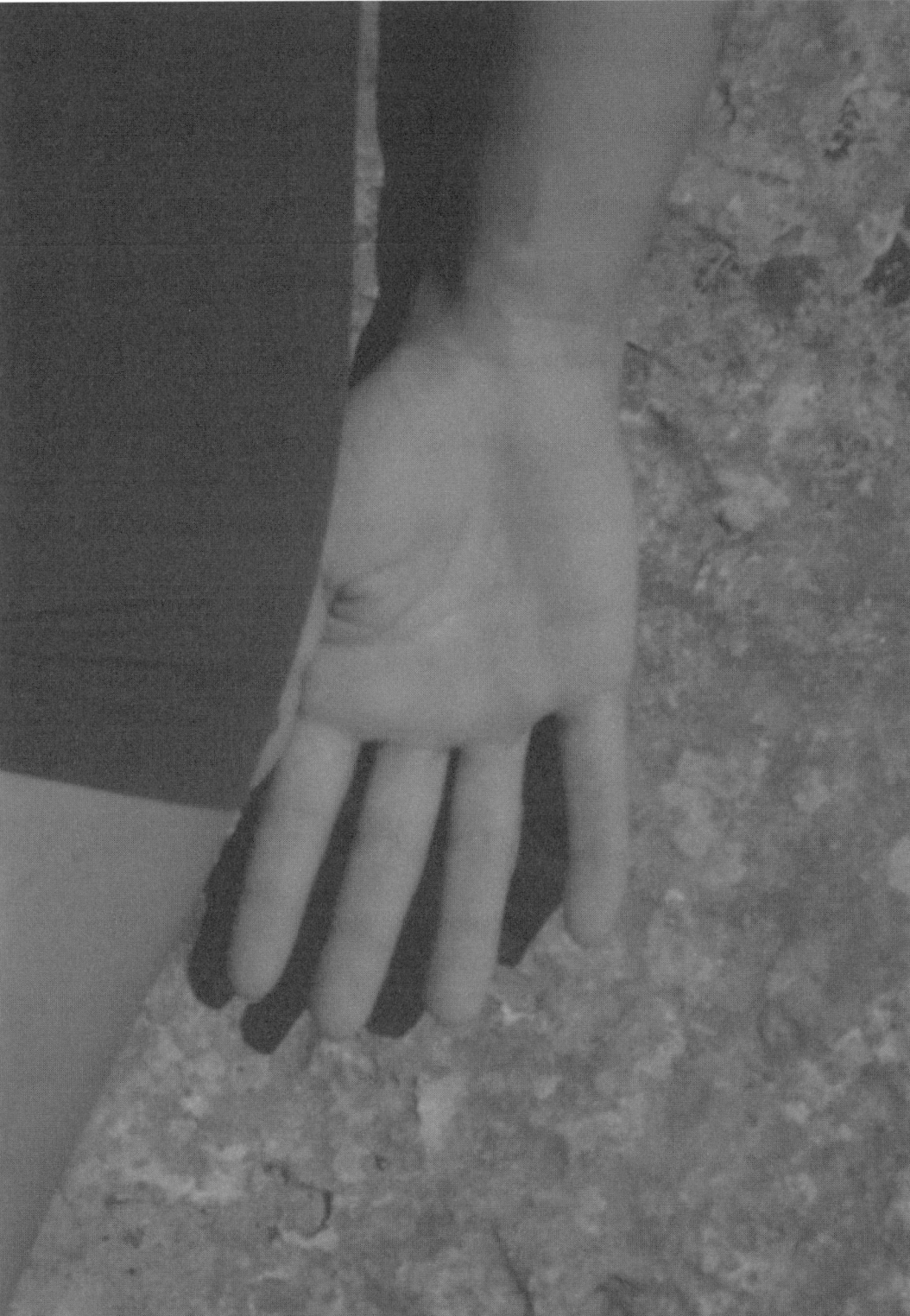

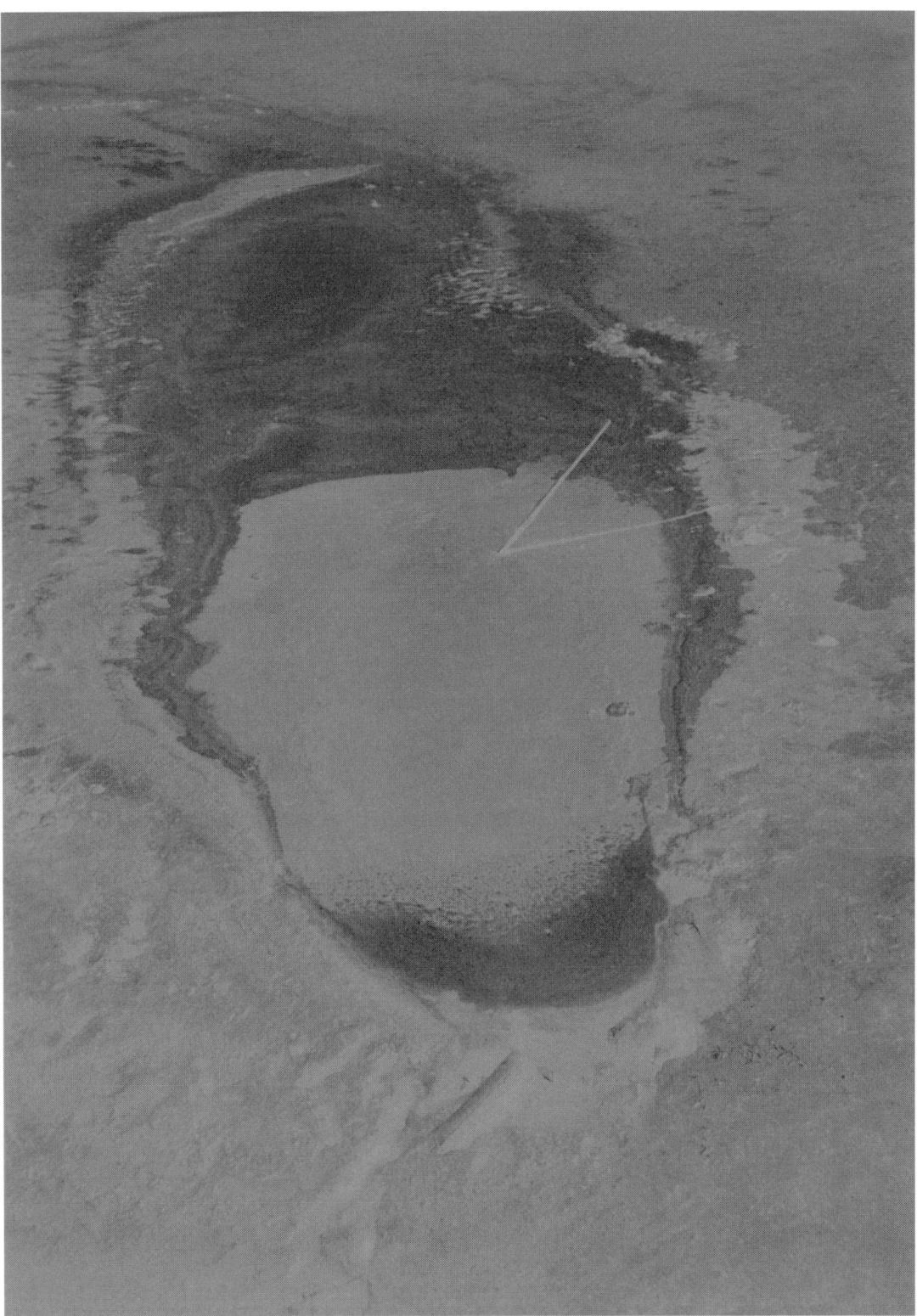

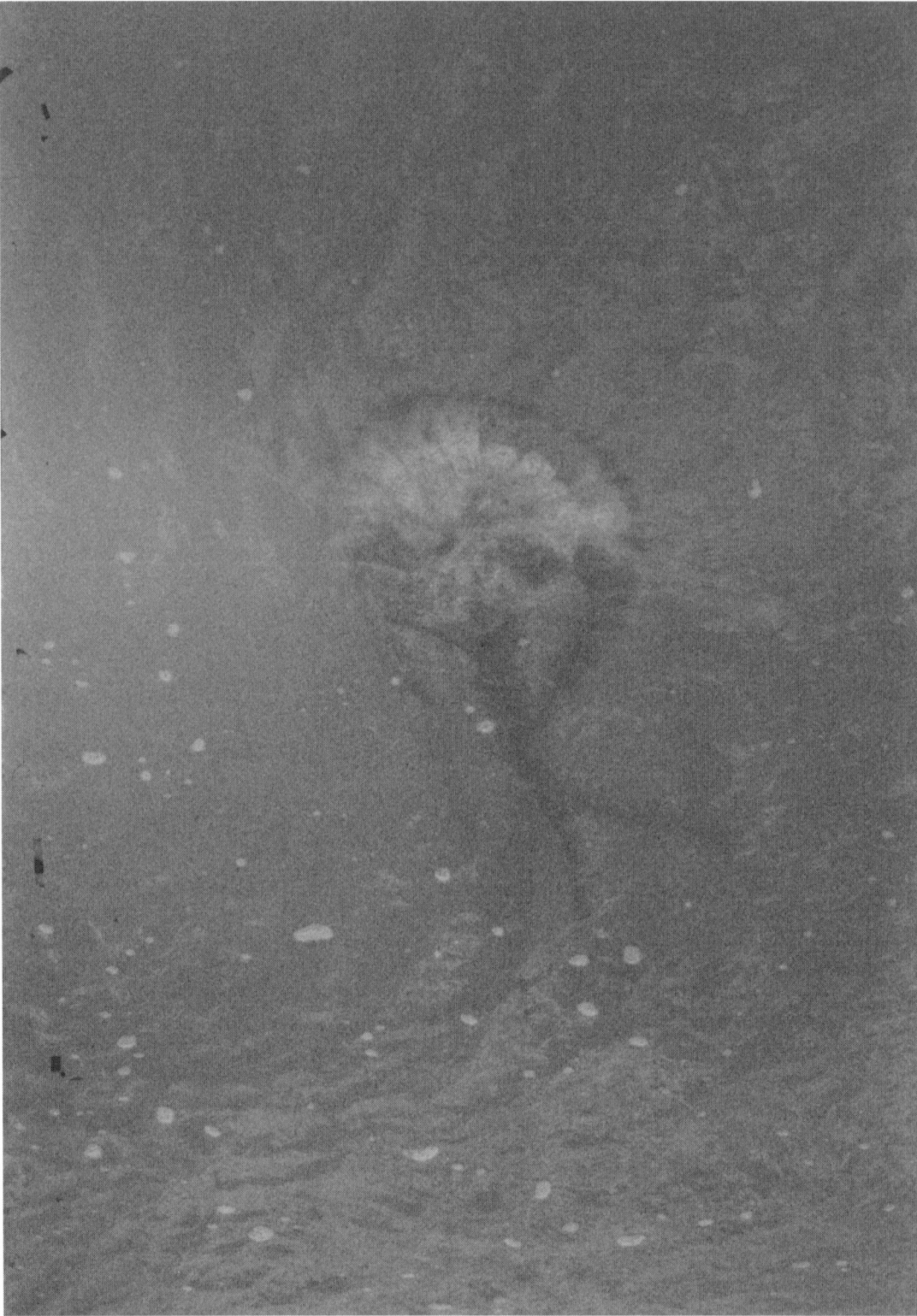

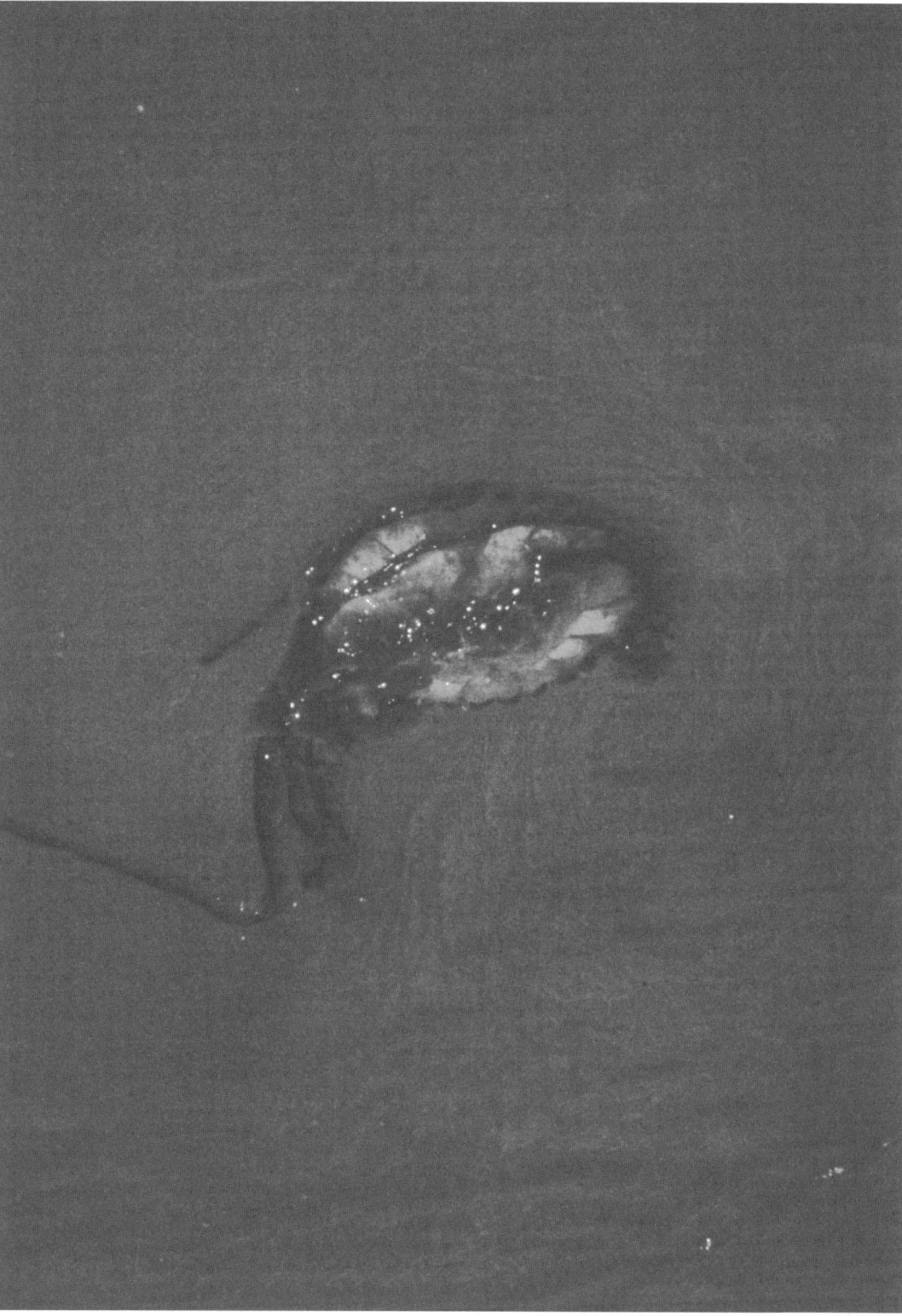

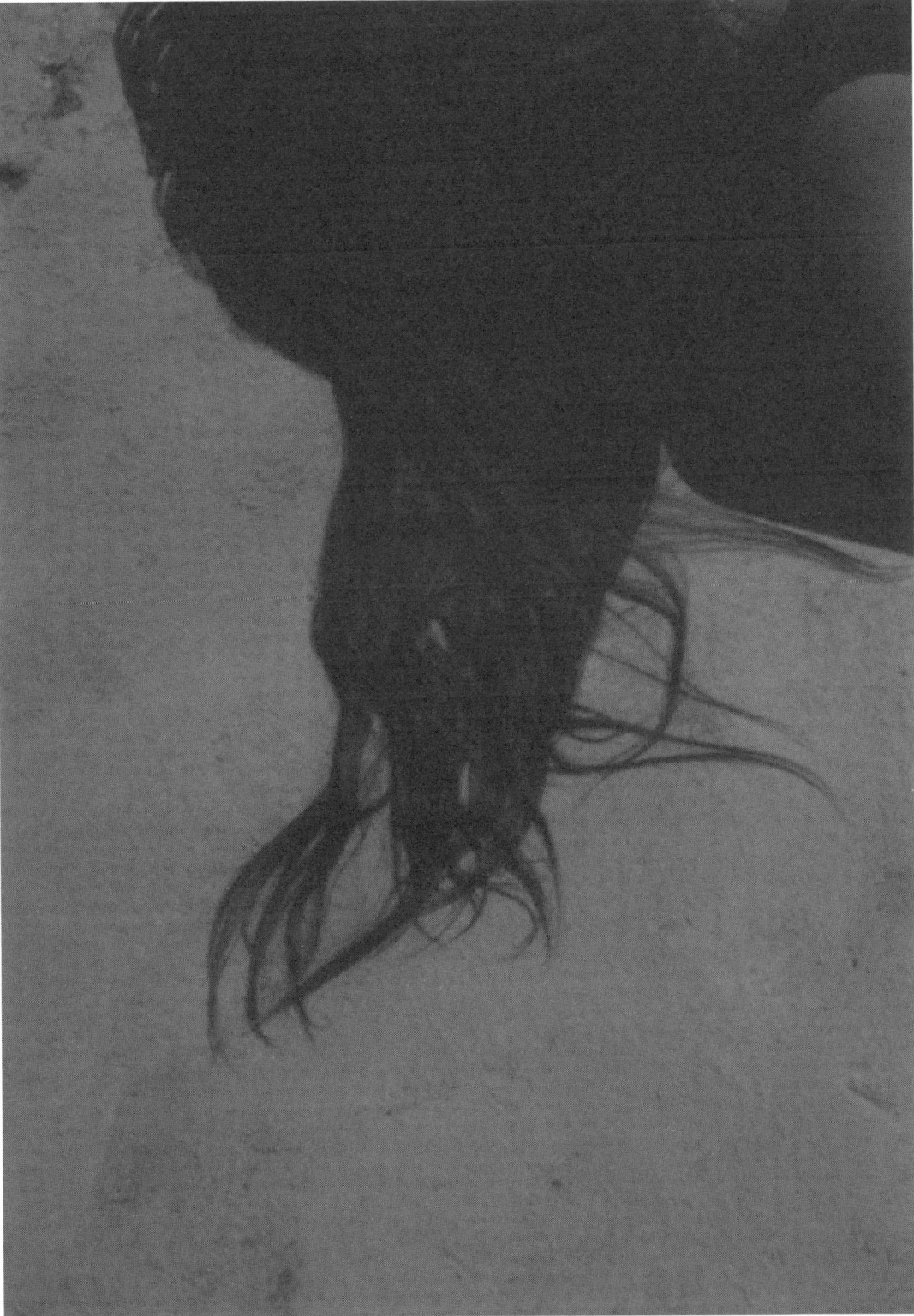

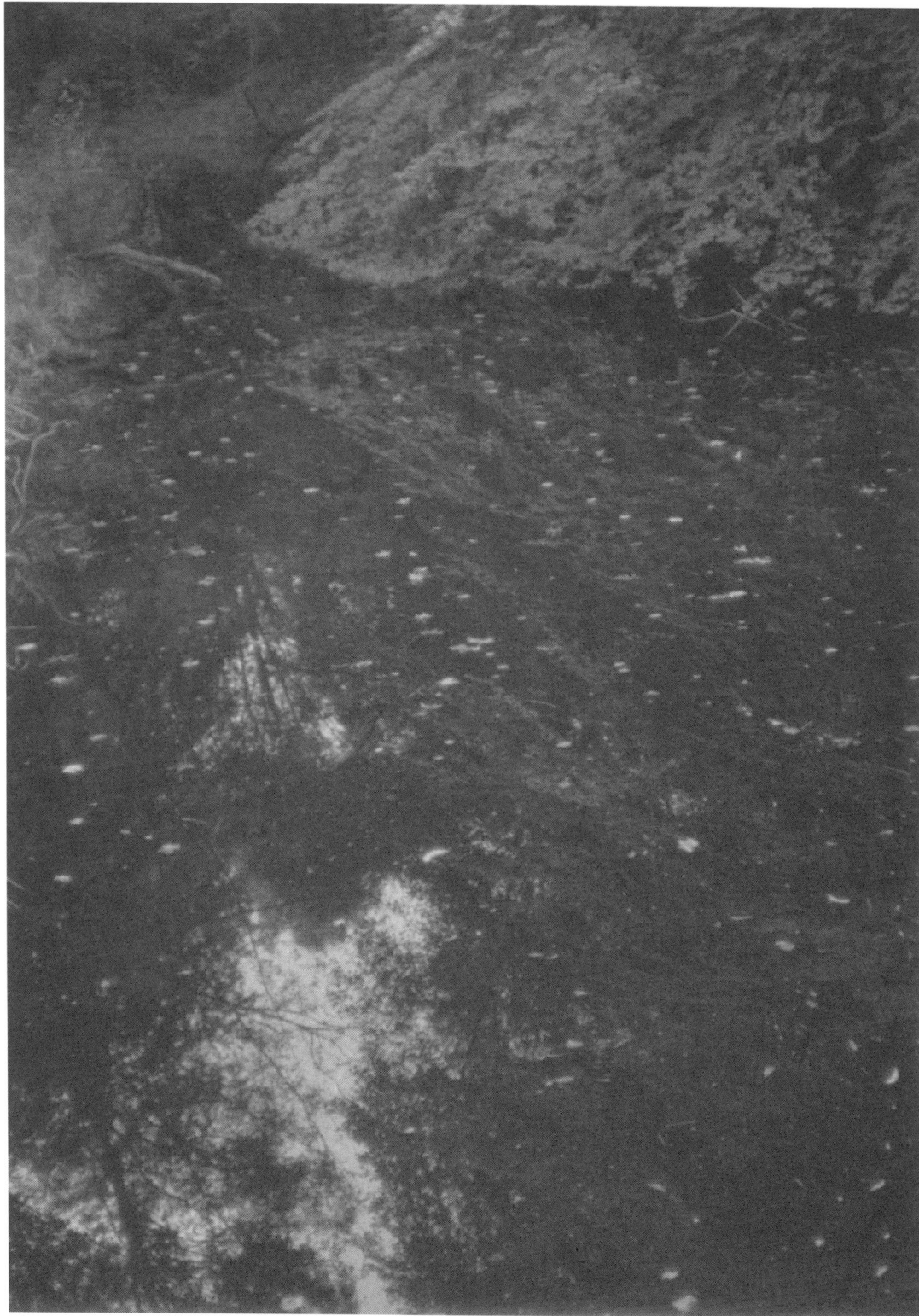

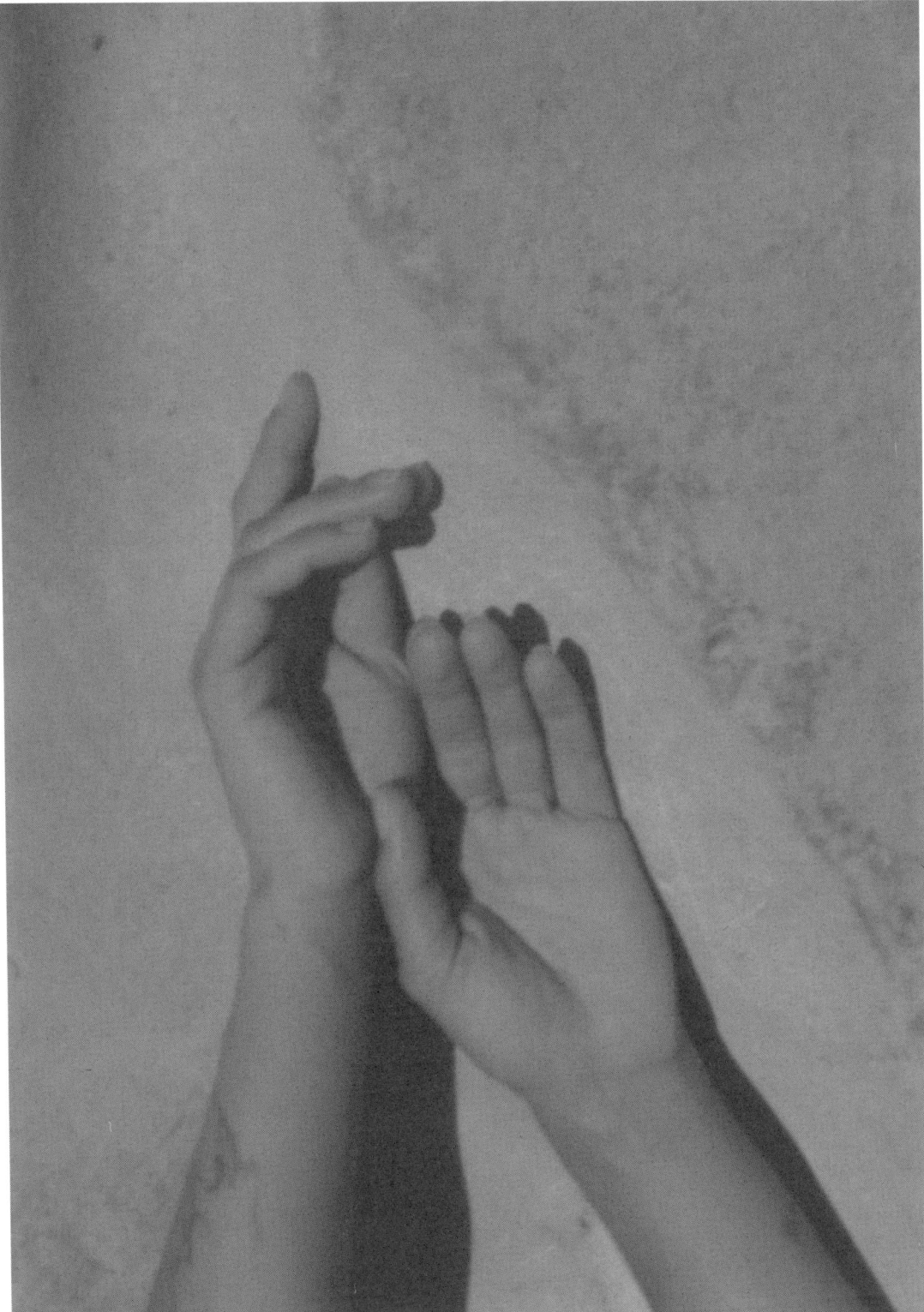

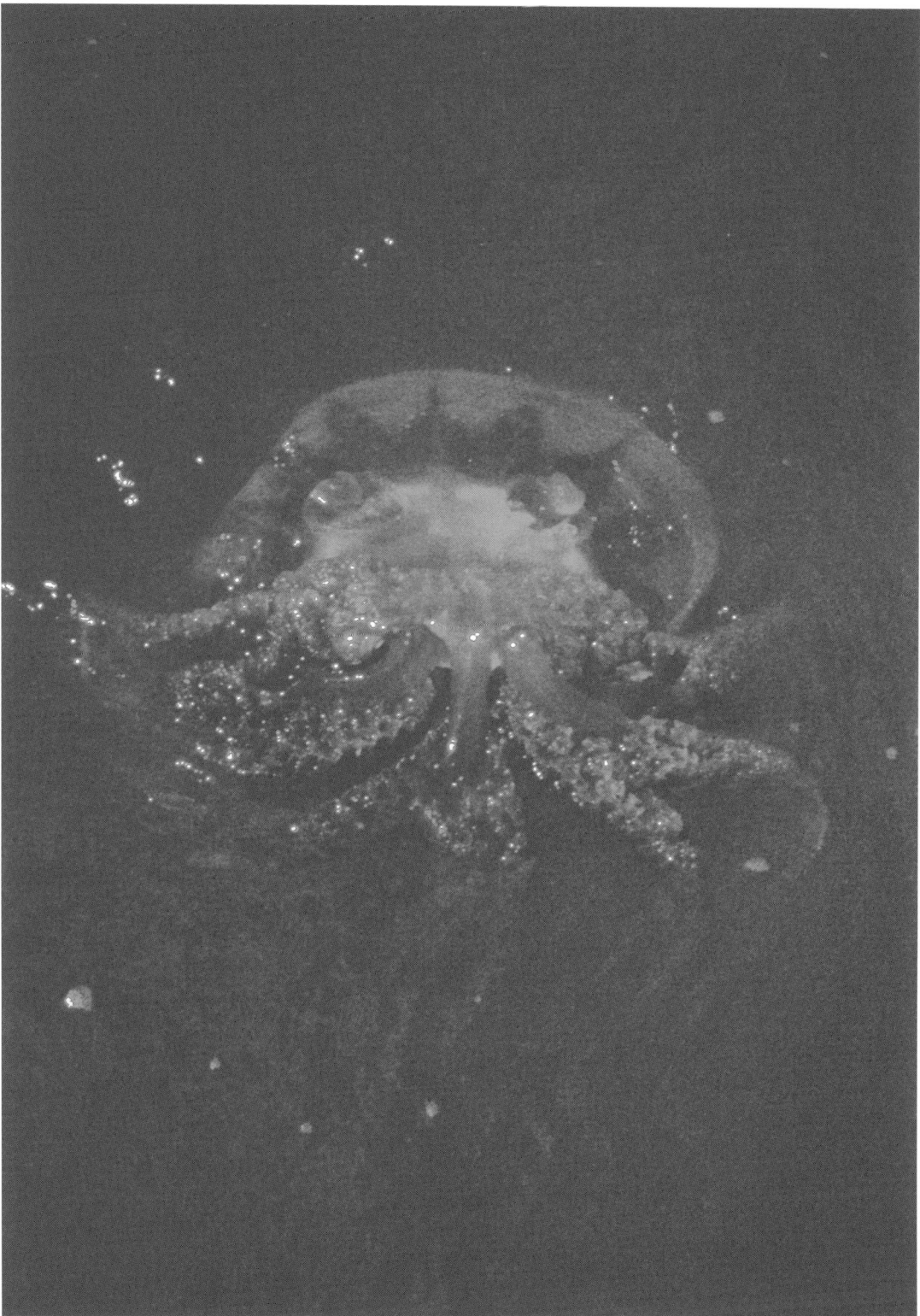

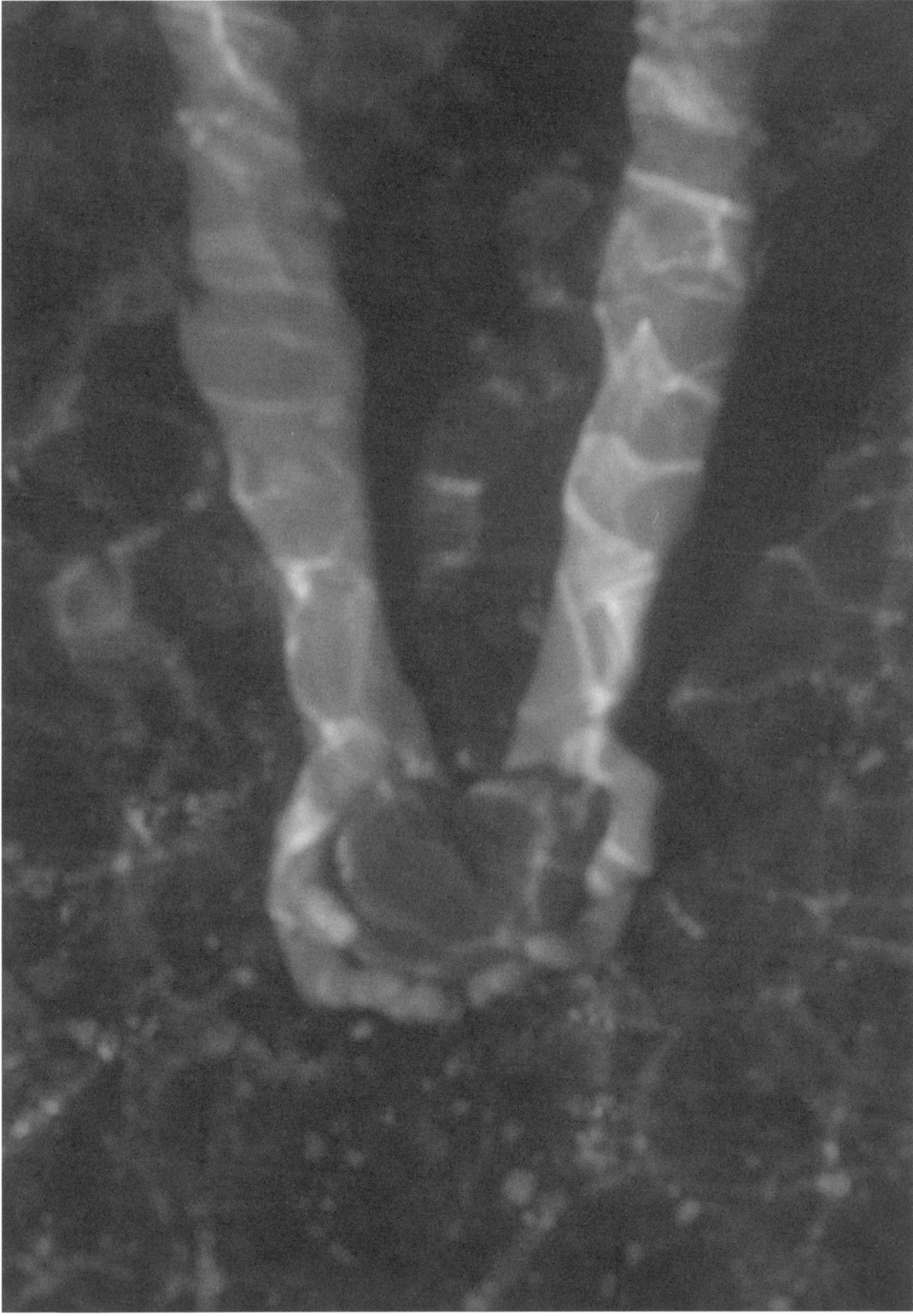

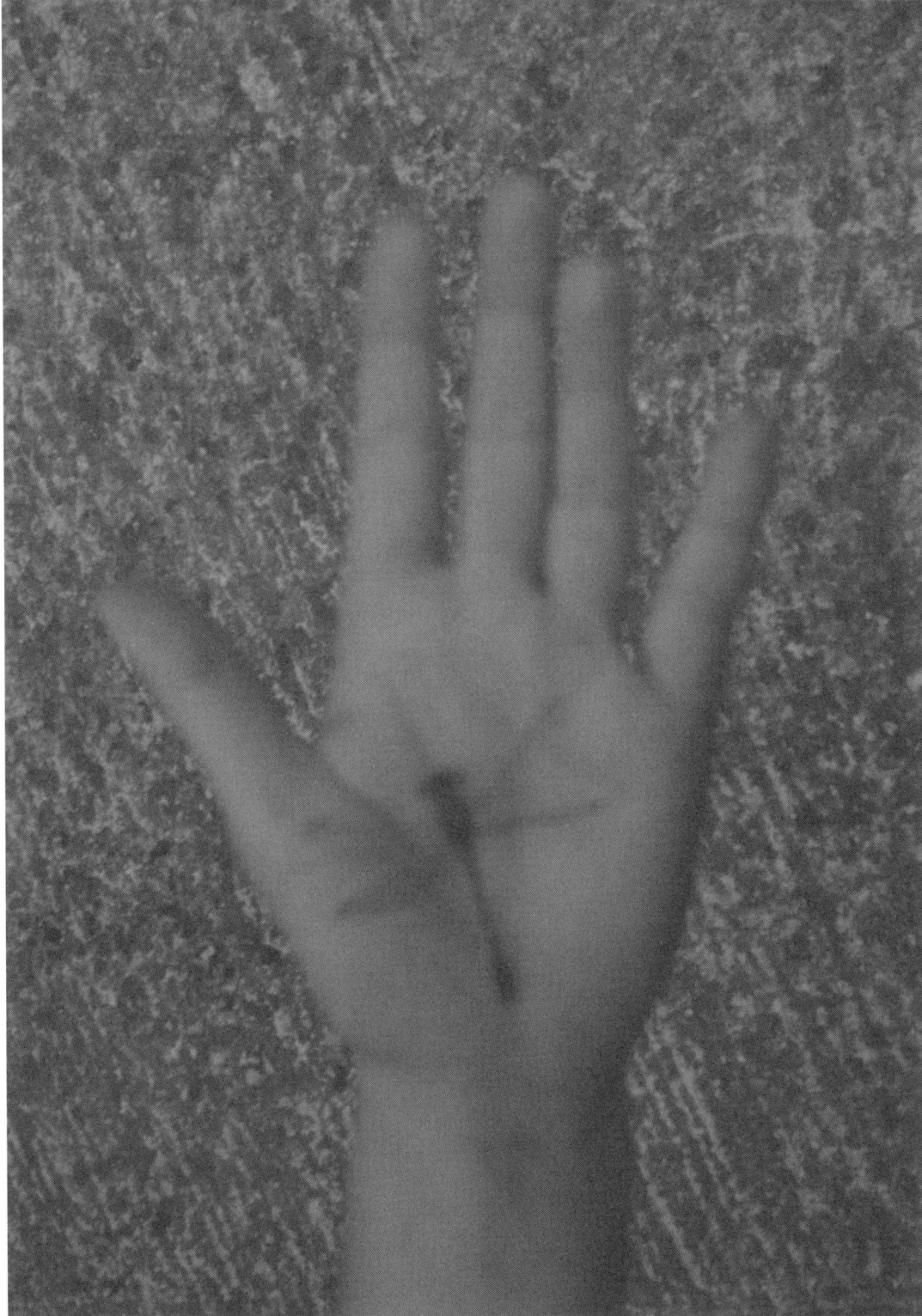

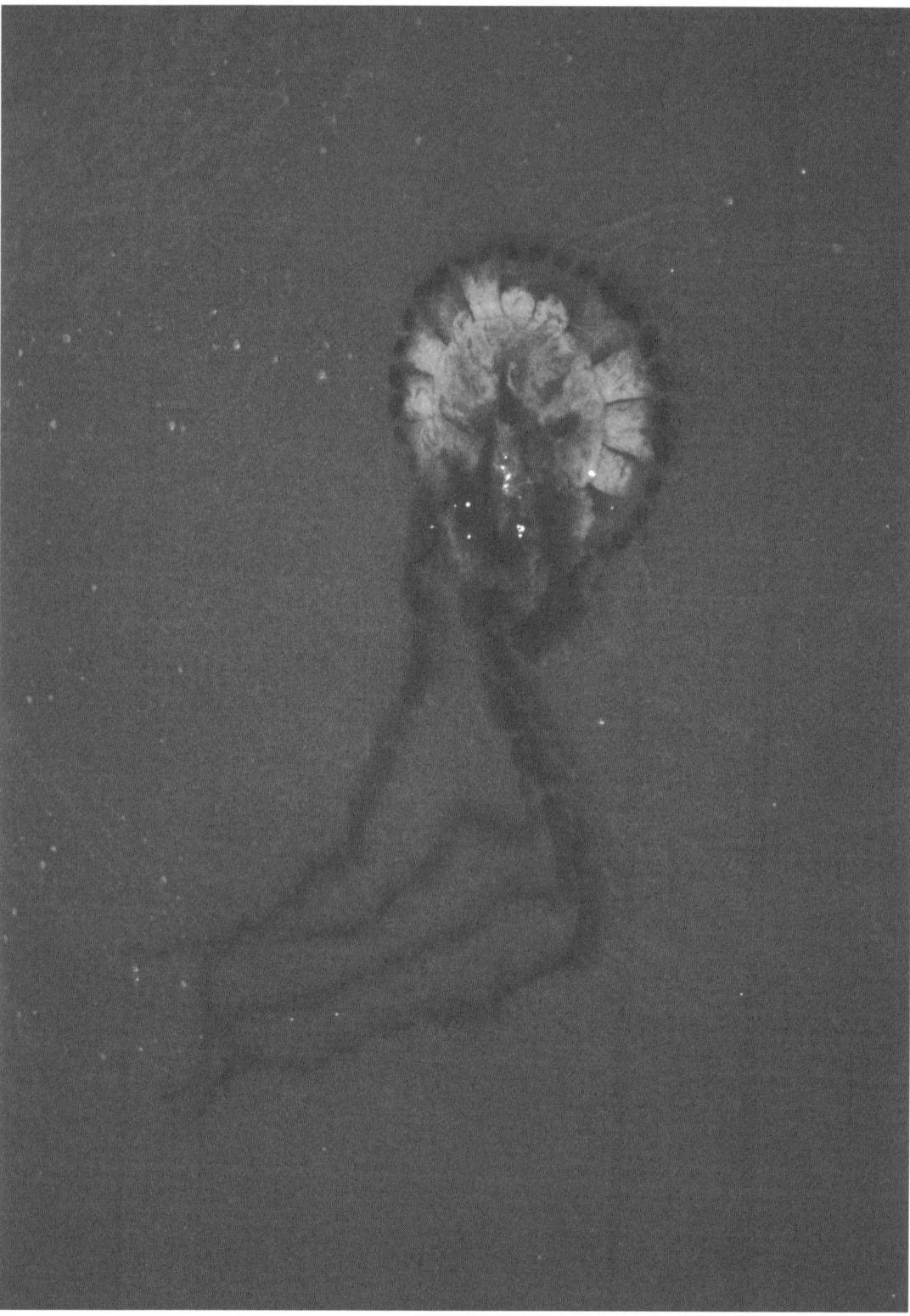

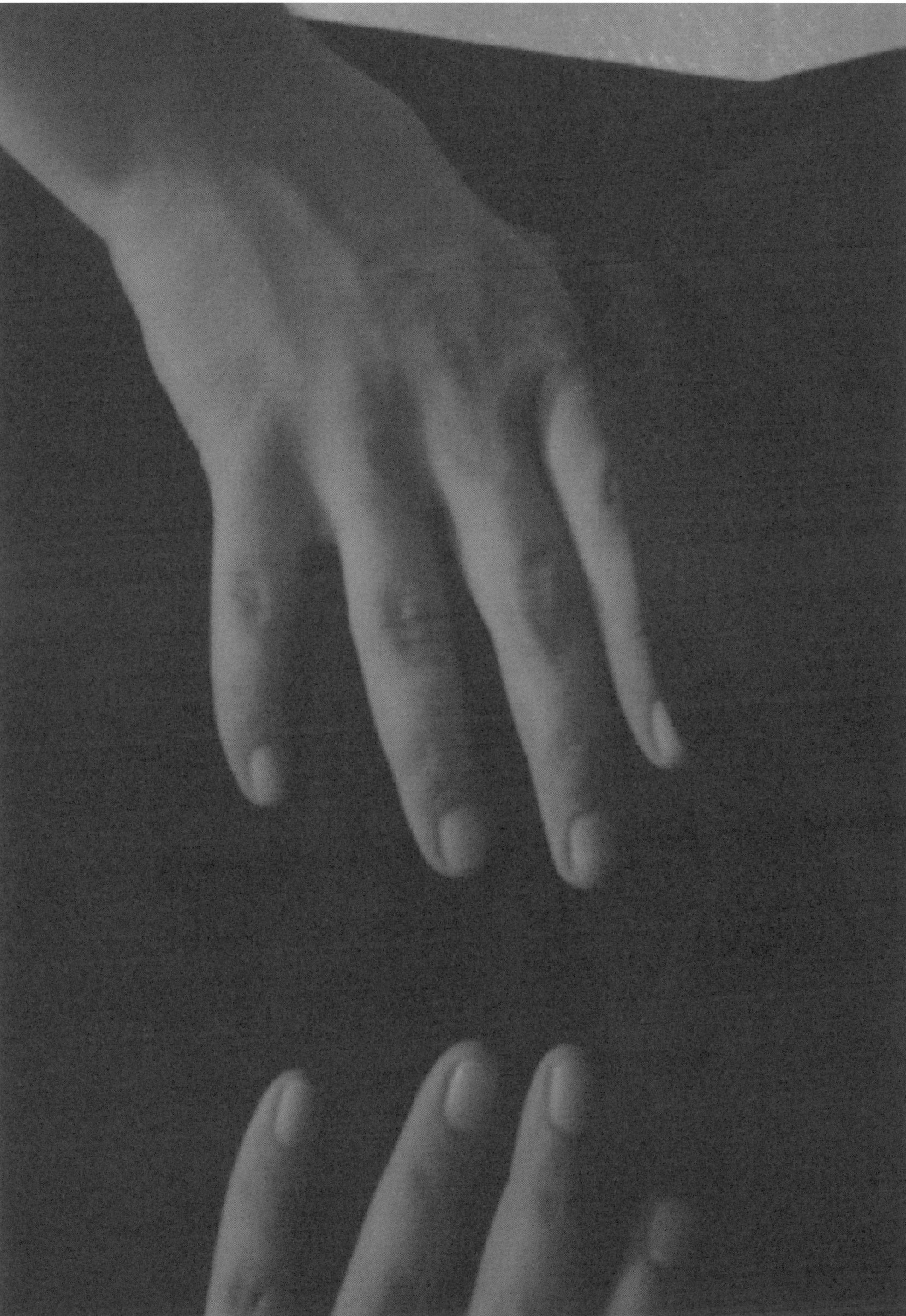

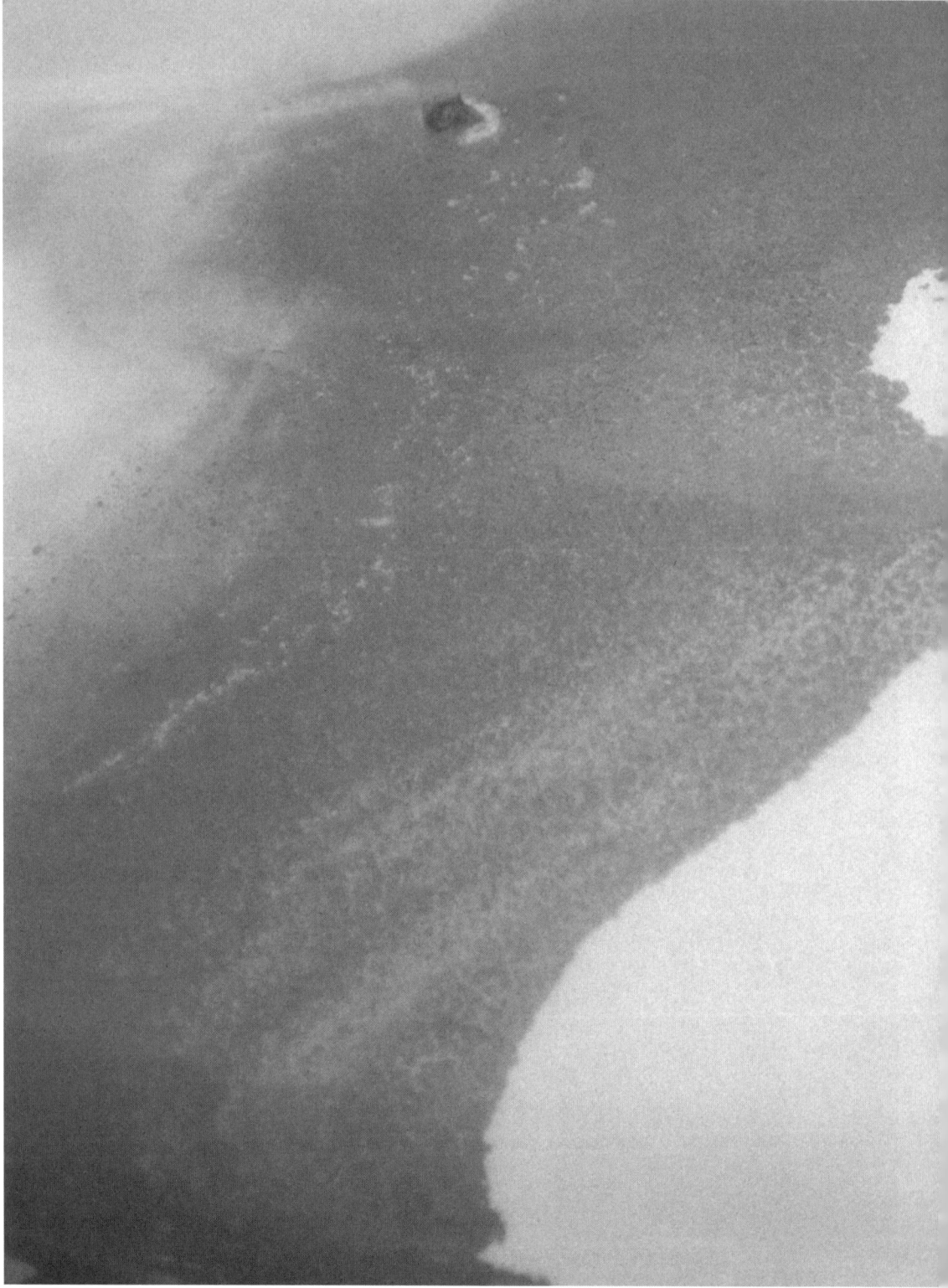

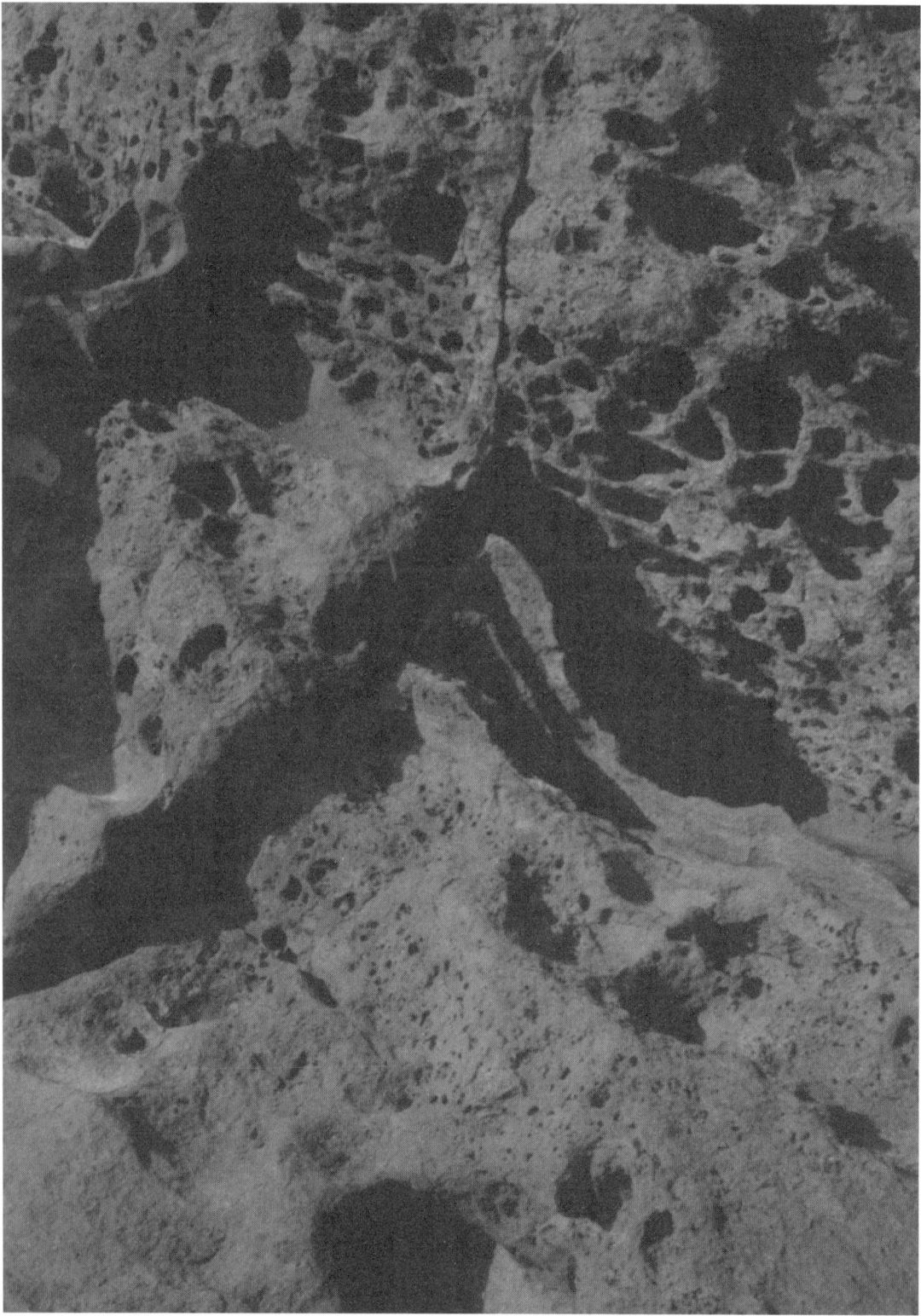

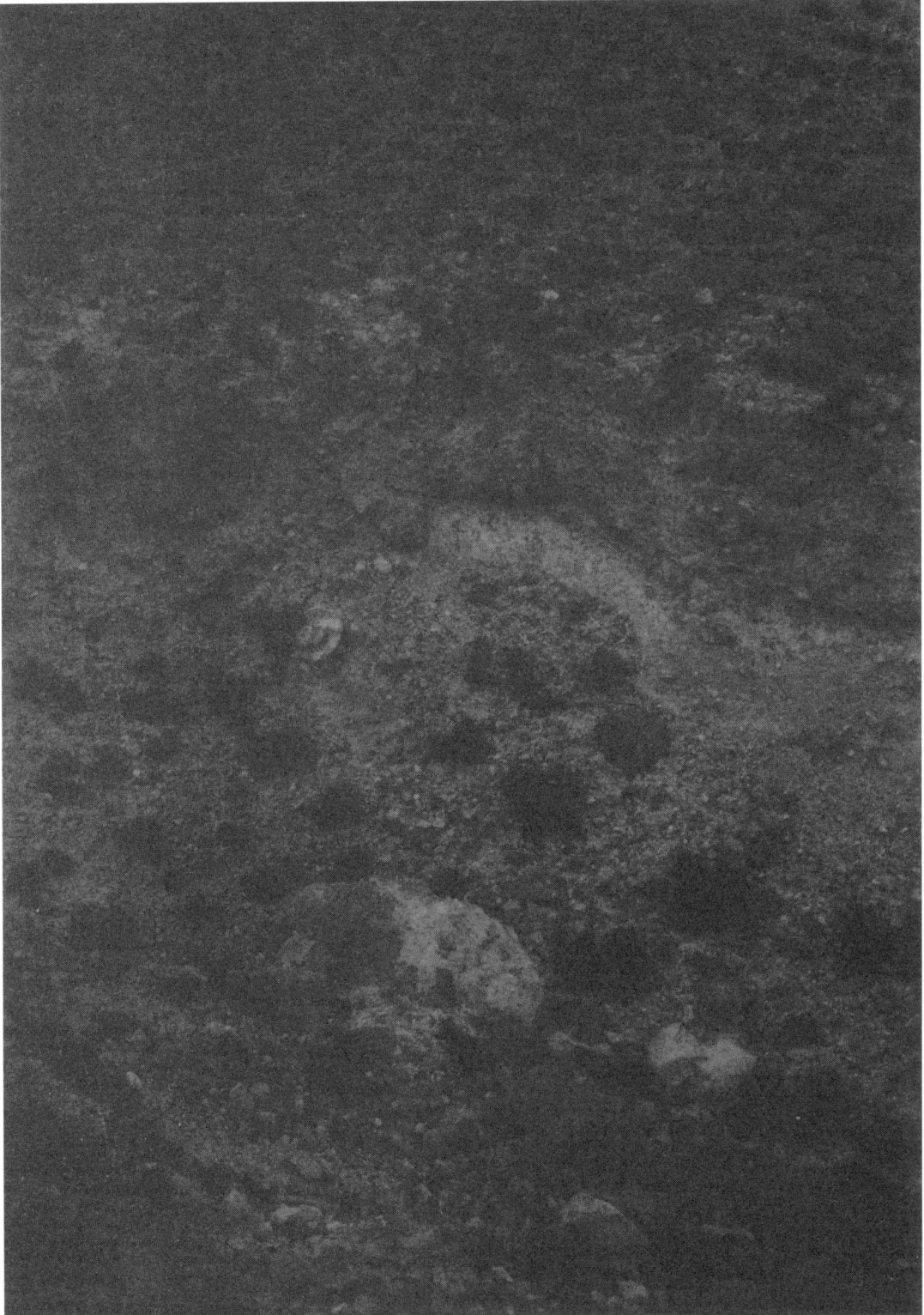

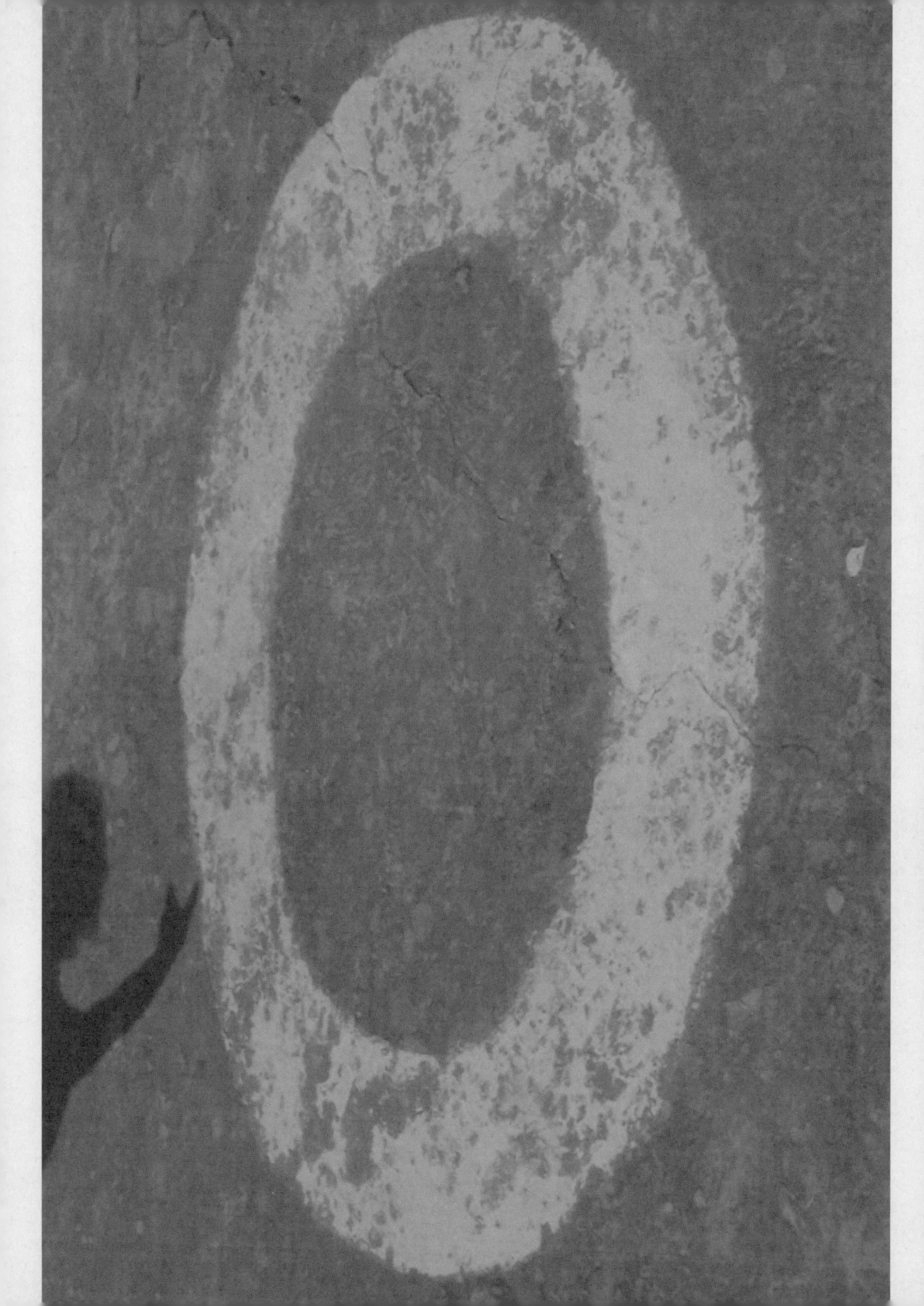

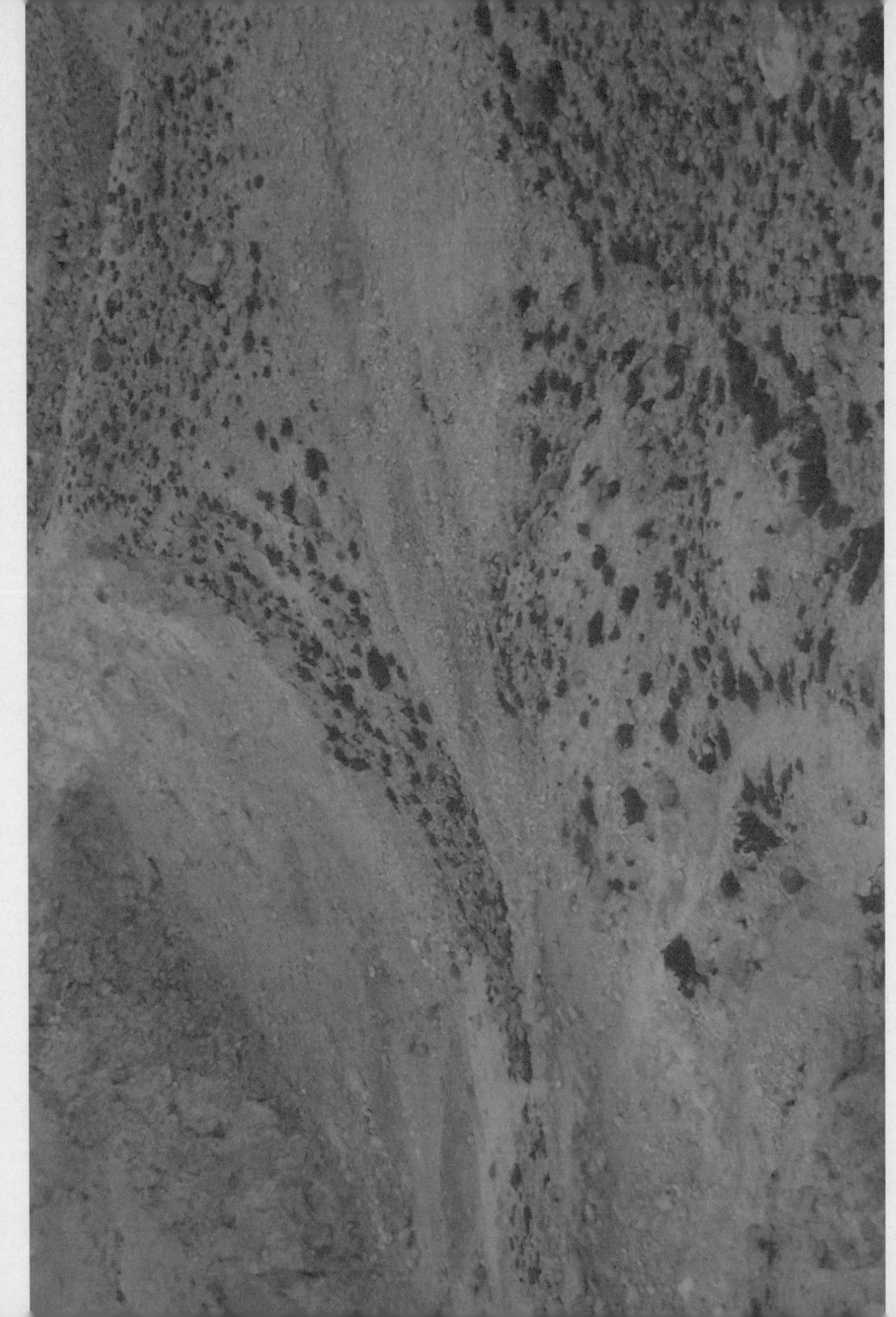

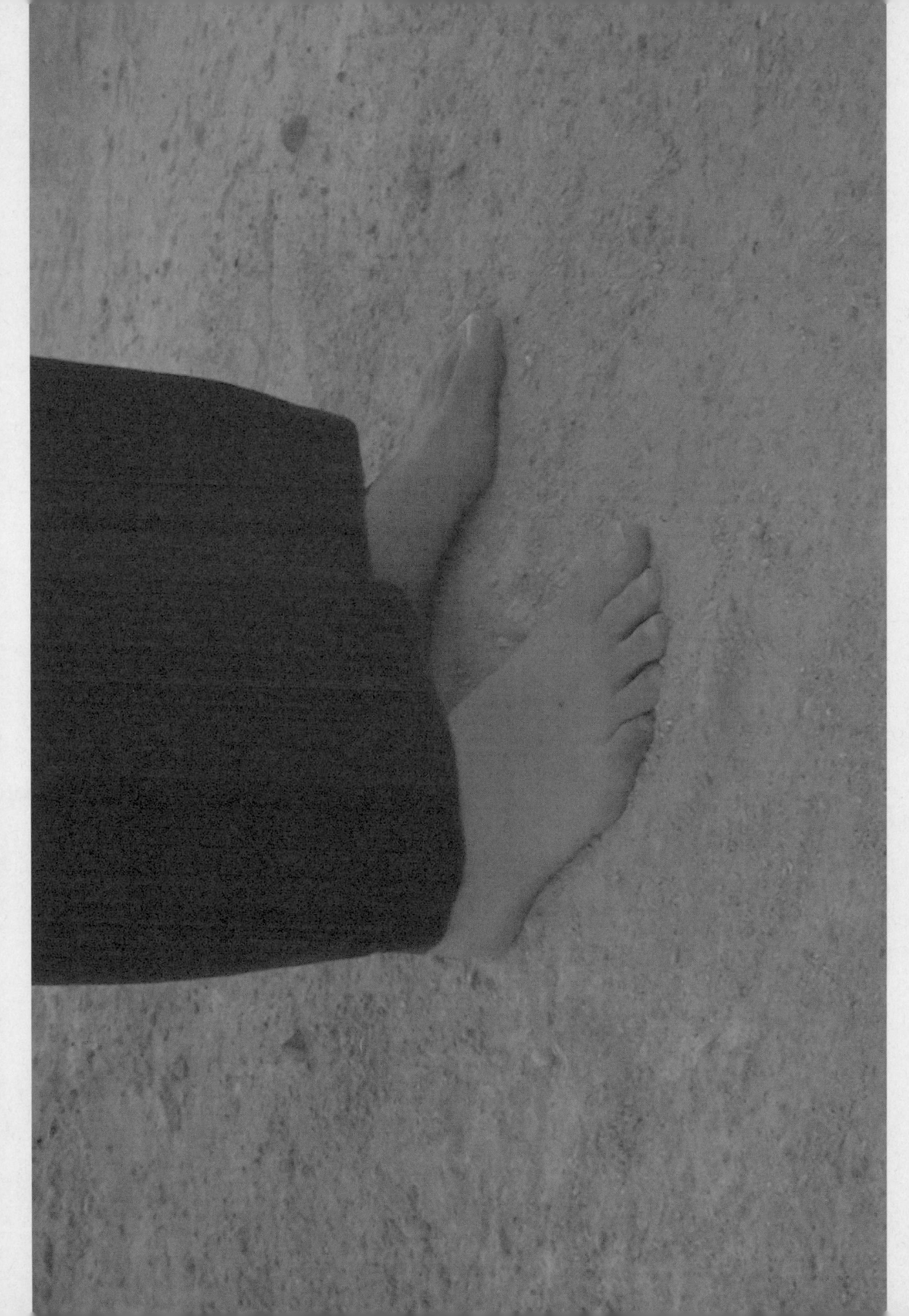

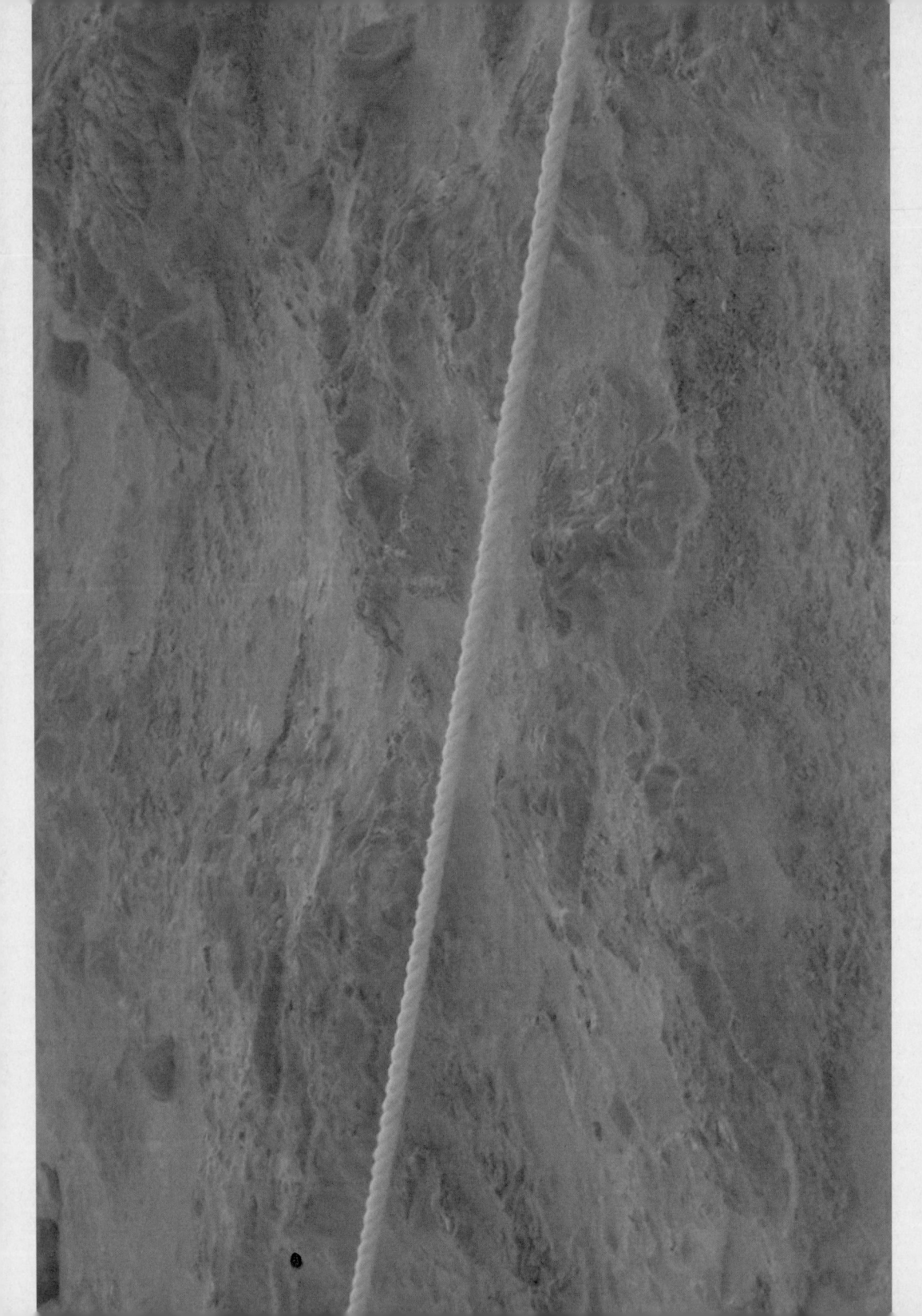

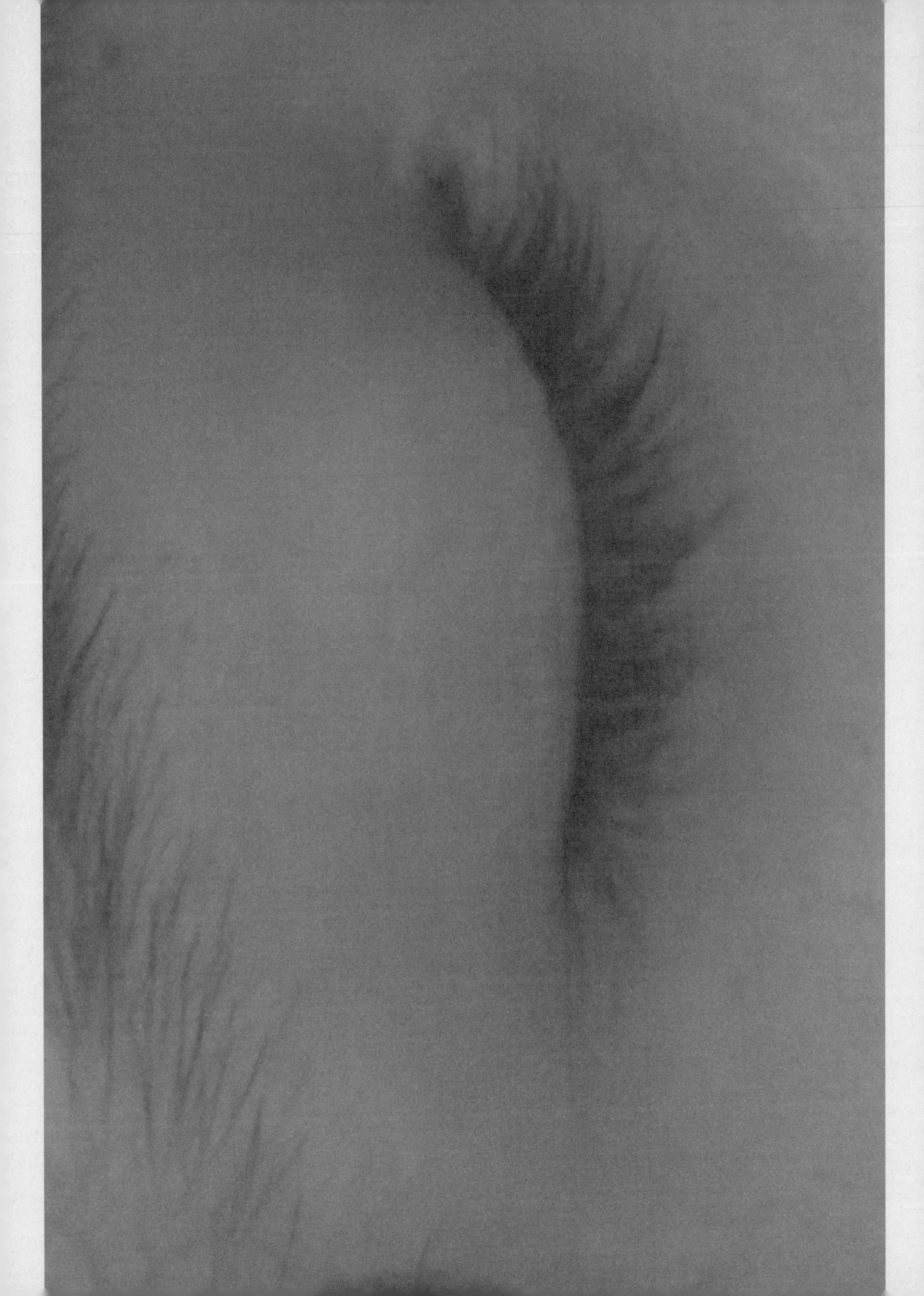

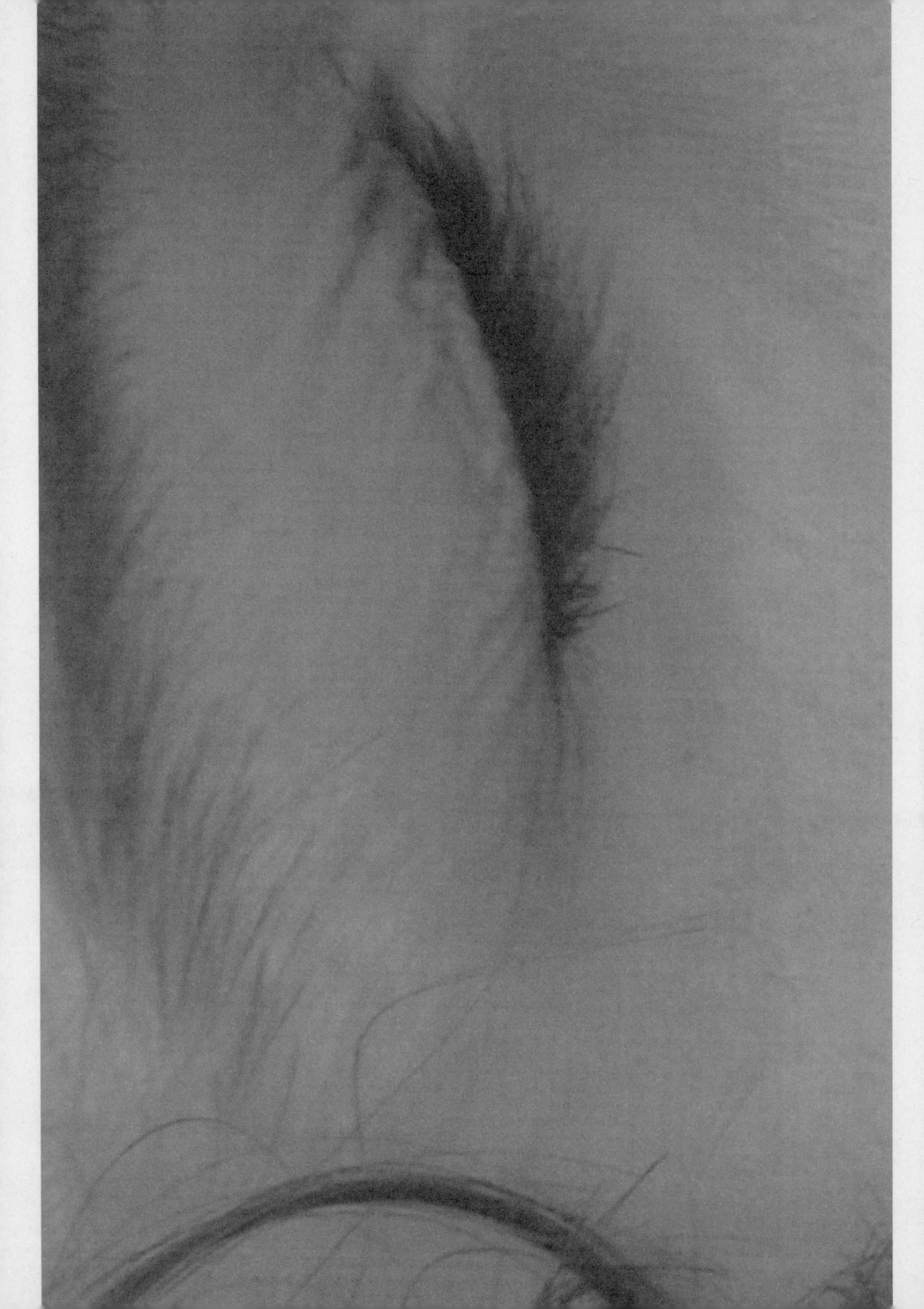

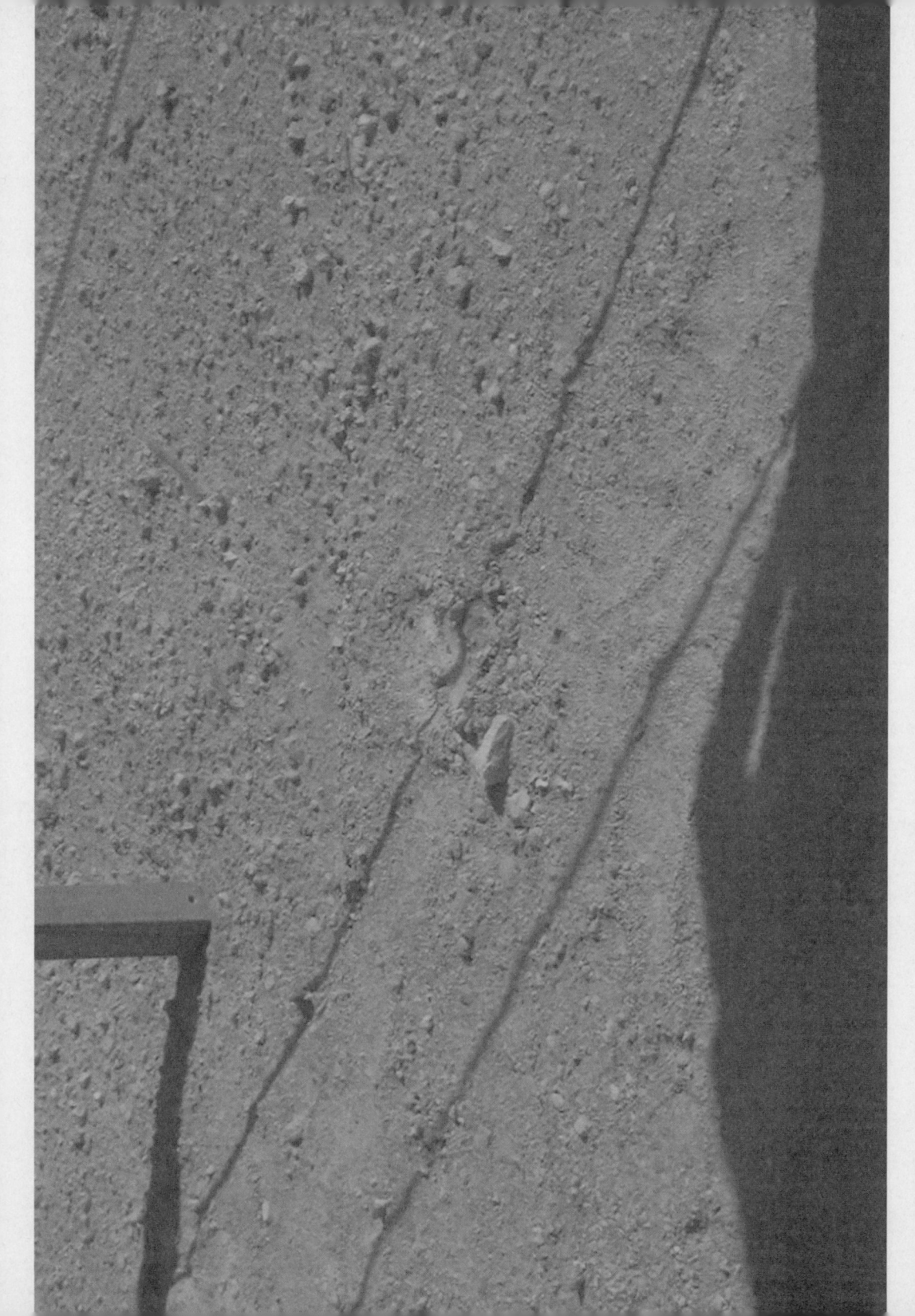

C. 2024
Eliot Nasrallah and Kult Books

First edition of 400 copies
ISBN 978-91-987607-3-6

Book design by Eliot Nasrallah
and Janne Riikonen

Printing and binding
by Tallinn Book Printers

kultbooks.com

I would like to thank Flore Gaboreau,
Nina Overkott, Carmen Woreth,
Timothée Charon, Gisèle Ghanem,
Janne Riikonen, Juliette Hage,
Ralph Nasrallah, Noémie Graciani,
Swann Bossé and Rotolux Press
for their help with the book project.

LES YEUX FERMÉS

(the volcano song)

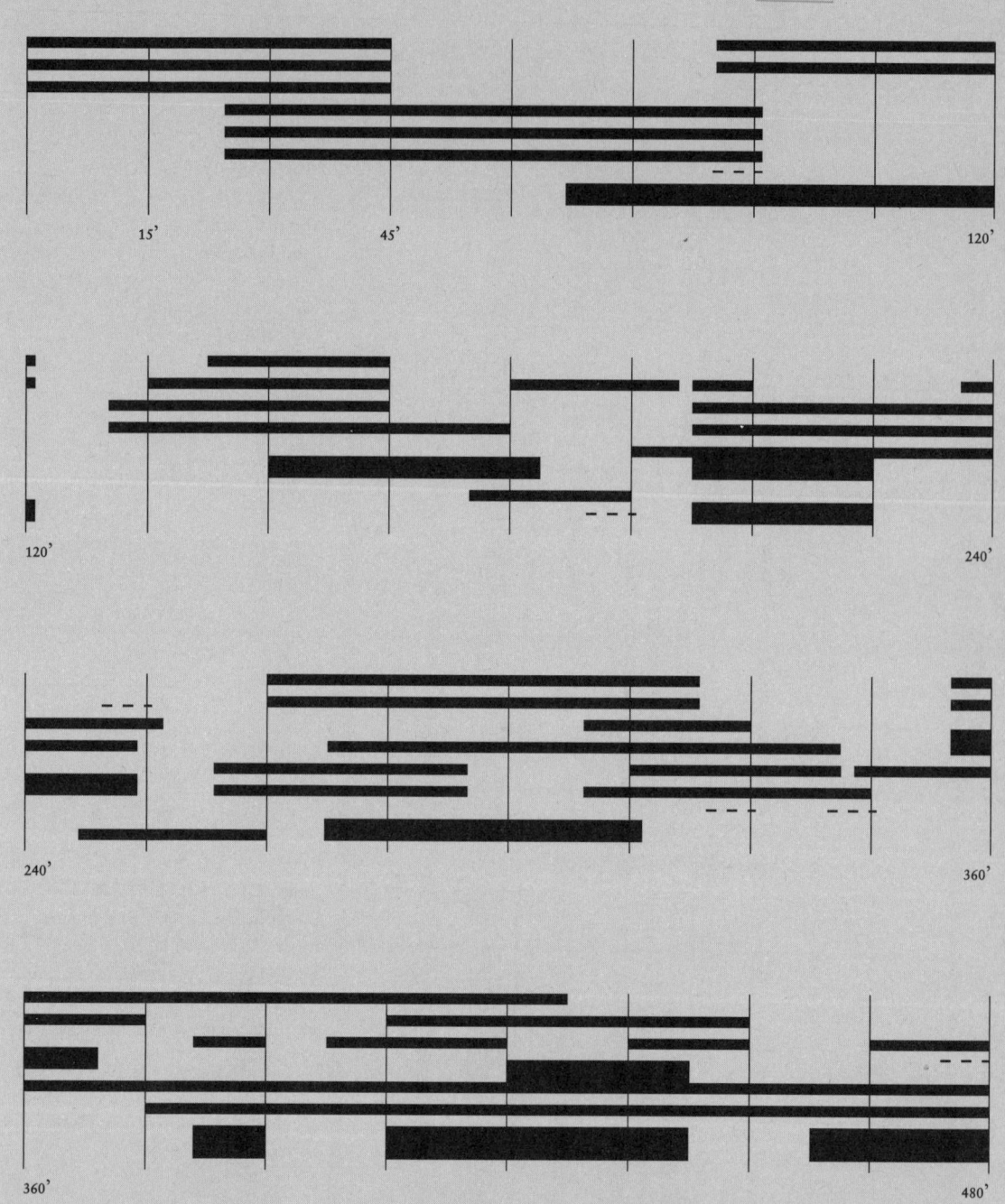